D1551570

NEW BELIEVERS

A Four-Week Study Guide

Christopher J. Weeks

CONTENTS

"What just happened?" For well over 25 years in ministry, I have come across countless numbers of people in the church and outside the church that have said these exact words after making a personal decision to begin following Jesus Christ. Some of those people responded to God after hearing a moving sermon, others committed to Jesus after going to a Christian music conference, and I have even met some who were walking in the woods by themselves where they encountered the Living God. And yet they are desperate to understand what happened. I have come to realize that there are scores of professing believers that still have no idea what it means to be a Christian or why they suddenly feel compelled to grow deeper in their walk with Christ. If you have ever wondered what it means to truly believe then this study was written with you in mind and I want to help you be clear on where you are now standing with God and how to move forward with Jesus.

This booklet is designed in an easy to use four-week study guide format. I know people are not all scholars and are often terrified about jumping into something that is way over their heads. I want to make his Word easy and accessible to all people. My hope is that in less than a month, which is a relatively short amount of time, you will be able to gain certainty on the most important life decision a person could ever make; their salvation. So whether you are a new believer, an unsure believer, or even a long time believer that was never really sure of your position with Christ, I want to encourage you that it is never too late to get real with God.

This four-week study is meant to be both clear and concise so you will not be confused about what it means to be an actual follower of Christ. The topics will range from discussing what you did when you accepted Jesus to how it will affect the rest of your life, but my greatest hope is that you will be assured that Jesus is actually and truly your God for all eternity. Even after you complete this booklet you may still have hundreds of questions about Christianity, but hopefully, not about your decision to make Jesus Lord of your life. As the late Peter Marshall once said, "Following Jesus offers the greatest adventure for those who dare becoming explorers of things related to heaven and eternity." And there's no time like the present to begin that incredible adventure!

❖ *This study is going to discuss the essentials of Christianity and to get the full impact of this study, it is recommended that you ask a mature believer to walk alongside you so they can help you traverse some of the difficult Biblical terminology and resource tools. Also, if you don't already own or possess a Bible, look for one that is easy to read and follow. Some of the preferred versions are the New International Version (NIV), the English Standard Version (ESV), or the New Living Translation (NLT). If you do not have access to one, ask a local church or go to a local Bible bookstore to purchase one. There are also many wonderful free Bible apps available online that you can download to any mobile device.*

.

WEEK ONE

Understanding Your Decision

Authentic Christianity is the whole goal of this book. And to reach this goal, honest self-evaluation is a must. Feeling, passion, and "being caught up in the moment" fades fast, but genuine life-transformation lasts forever. As you begin this journey to know Christ, you must look at why you have come to him. In John 1:38, Jesus turned to two men that wanted to follow him and asked, "What do you want?" Do you know why you want to follow him?

That is the purpose of this week's study: To help you. . .

> ▸ STEP ONE: Re-Examine Your Decision
>
> ▸ STEP TWO: Find the Biblical Basis of Salvation
>
> ▸ STEP THREE: Reaffirm Your Commitment to Christ

▶ <u>STEP ONE: Re-Examine Your Decision</u>

Write out, in the space provided, the decision you made, why you accepted Jesus as your Savior, and what you exactly said or did:

After making the decision to accept Christ how do you feel about it now? Was it the right one, are you sure you still want Jesus as your God?

Do you think this decision you made was something you want to try for a while and see if it sticks, or is it something you know will change your life forever?

♀ The preceding questions are very important, and if you need to rethink them, do it now.

Many people make decisions for a lot of wrong reasons which could tragically keep someone in ignorance and on their way to damnation. Read 1 Corinthians 15:2 and write down what you think it means in your own words.

So to make you fully aware of what it means to "Accept Christ as your Savior", or to "Invite him into your heart", we must fully understand what we have gotten into.

▶ STEP TWO: Find the Biblical Basis of Salvation

The Bible is our authority for what we believe and live by. It is not smart people or emotional experiences that determine truth, but spiritual realities are authenticated by the Bible alone. Look at 2 Timothy 3:15-16 and put it into your own words.

If the Bible says one thing and a man or woman you respect says something completely opposite of the Bible, which one should you believe and why?

So, according to the AUTHORITY of the Bible...

1. What actually happened when you accepted Christ?

♀ YOU WERE SAVED

What do you think the word saved means?

What do you think you were saved from?

Romans 5:9 says what?

Ephesians 2:3-5 says what?

_____

_____

_____

_____

Read John 5:24 and then answer the following questions:

What happens if you don't believe?

_____

_____

_____

What does it mean to be condemned?

_____

_____

_____

If you believed, what kind of place are you now residing?

_____

_____

_____

After reading these verses, what do you think it means to be saved?

_____

_____

_____

♀ YOU WERE BORN AGAIN

What do you think being born again means?

Do you think you have to be a religious wild man to be born again?

John 3:3-8 says what

John 1:12-13 says what?

Read Titus 3:3-7 and answer the following questions:

Did God save us because of anything we have done?

What do you think the washing of rebirth means?

So who was poured out on us and what does that mean?

How important is it to be born again?

♀ YOU WERE BOUGHT BY JESUS TO BE HIS SLAVE

Do you like the idea that you are someone's slave?

If Jesus never bought you, do you think you would be a slave to anyone else? (See Romans 6:17-18)

1 Corinthians 6:19-20 says what?

How much do you think that price was according to. . .

Psalm 49:7-8

1 Peter 1:18-19

How does God want to treat you according to John 15:15?

So if God bought you out of slavery from sin and Satan, and He wants to treat you as a friend, how does that make you feel concerning your relationship with him?

2. How will the decision you made for Jesus affect the rest of your life?

♀ I NO LONGER LIVE HOW I USE TO

Galatians 2:20 says what?

_____

_____

_____

_____

What do you think it means when it says that Christ "lives" in me?

_____

_____

_____

Do you think that having Christ live in you will make a difference in your life?

_____

_____

_____

What kind?

_____

_____

Here is what your life once was like and here is what it should look like now:

COLOSSIANS 3:5-17

Write down how your life should be different now that you are a follower of Christ:

_____

_____

_____

_____

How should you expect your old friends to treat you according to 1 Peter 4:3-5?

_____

_____

_____

So according to what you have just read concerning how your life will be different; does it sound like Christianity will be a fun and easy life? Why or why not?

_____

_____

_____

_____

_____

3. How you can be assured that Jesus will be your God forever.

♀ HE GIVES YOU A GUARANTEE

Read Ephesians 1:13-14 and answer the following questions:

What happens to you immediately after you believe?

_____

_____

_____

What do you think that means?

According to this verse, why is the Holy Spirit given to you?

_____

_____

_____

How secure do you think a guarantee is with the Almighty God according to Hebrews 6:18?

_____

_____

_____

What does John 10:27-30 say?

How strong do you think God's grip is?

So do you think if you have really become a child of God, that God will ever lose you?

According to Colossians 1:13, what kingdom do you now live in if you are truly a Christian?

Do you think you will lose your citizenship according to Philippians 3:20-21?

FINAL NOTE: What encourages you the most about knowing that your future is secure in God?

_____

_____

_____

_____

_____

_____

_____

▶ STEP THREE: Reaffirm Your Commitment to Christ

THE BIG QUESTION: Since you have just learned Christianity is not going to be a nice and easy life, do you still want to continue on with the decision you made to accept Jesus as your Savior knowing that it will cost you a lot?

_____

_____

_____

Why or why not?

_____

_____

_____

_____

If you answered yes, sign the following contract. . .

Dear Lord Jesus Christ,

On this day _____, I agree to commit my life fully to you as your child and friend. I know that what you have saved me from is my slavery to sin and eternal damnation. Because of this, I am willing to fully obey your word, allow other Christians in my life and put up with what ever hardship comes my way. I recognize that following you will be at times very difficult, and with your help I will press on – you deserve it!

Signed: _____

WEEK TWO

Importance of Spiritual Food

Hopefully, from the last week's discussion, you have understood the idea of being "Born Again". And just as a new child needs good food to physically grow in good health, a new spiritual child needs good spiritual food to spiritually grow up in Christ. By the time you are done with this lesson you should be able to develop fundamental habits that you can carry with you the rest of your life – and if you continue in these habits, they WILL rebound in praise and honor to Christ!

That is the purpose of this weeks' study: To help you understand fully. . .

> ▶ STEP ONE: What Spiritual Food Is
>
> ▶ STEP TWO: How to Eat It and Grow From It
>
> ▶ STEP THREE: Setting Up Your Own Biblical Diet

▶ STEP ONE: What Spiritual Food Is

1. From the following verses, see if you can determine what you think God considers the necessary food you need to grow...

Matthew 4:4

1 Peter 2:2-3

1 Corinthians 3:1-2

Romans 10:17

♀ What is the food that God has provided for you?

2. Why is eating so important? This seems rather simple when you are talking about physical nourishment, but many Christians don't see the importance of knowing and understanding the Word. We must see why it is so important if we are really going to be motivated to use it.

IT IS ALIVE!! Read Hebrews 4:12 and then put it into your own words

_____

_____

_____

Why do you think it is important to read something that judges your thoughts and attitudes?

_____

_____

Can any other book cause you to change your behavior on a consistent basis that you know of?

_____

_____

And according to 2 Corinthians 3:17-18, how does the Bible change us?

_____

_____

IT TEACHES US HOW TO LIVE. What does 2 Timothy 3:15-16 say?

How does it say that the bible has come about?

What do you think that means?

Do you think the things the Bible talks about are pretty important if God wrote them? Why?

THE WORD OF GOD BRINGS US GOODNESS. Look at the following verses and write down the benefits of reading God's Word. . .

Joshua 1:8

Psalm 1:1-2

Luke 6:45

Psalm 119:98-100

Psalm 119:9

♀ What aspects of God's Word excites you the most?

♀ In your mind, is the Bible really that important? Why or why not?

▶ STEP TWO: How to Eat It and Grow From It

Eating is easy, right? Well, for many it is a learned art, just as it is for a baby eating its first piece of watermelon. It takes some time, but once you are used to it, it is a habit that becomes second nature. We will discuss four ways to eat the Word of God:

1. **General Reading**
2. **Studying (Word, Topic, Book)**
3. **Meditation**
4. **Memorization**

1. **General Reading**: The way to get used to it

In order to get familiar with different foods, you must first try them. Chomp on a steak and you will learn its texture, lick a Popsicle and you will feel the cold, crunch an apple and you will discover when it is fresh and when it is not. It is the same way with the Bible; just start reading it to learn how it reads.

As you read you will learn different stories, peoples and events. At first, they will be confusing, but soon you will realize that the Bible is one consistent story from start to finish. Here, let me give you an outline so you will have a basic idea what you are reading.

- Beginning of the World and Man (Genesis)

- History of God's People (Genesis through Nehemiah)

- Poetry and Songs (Job through Song of Songs)

- Prophets Warning Israel (Isaiah through Malachi)

- Jesus' Life (Matthew through John)

- Early Church (Acts)

- Letters to the followers of Jesus (Romans through Jude)

- End Time Events (Revelation)

At the beginning of the Bible, you will see the different books and you can pick where you would like to read. The key to growing is just to read, read, and read some more. If you never saw a football game before and then sat down and watched a game, do you think you would understand it all right away? You would hear terms like "line of scrimmage", or "offsides", or even "intentional grounding". The first time you heard these words you would say, "Wow, this is one confusing game--I don't understand!" or, "Boy, it is boring when you don't understand it." Many of you will say the same thing when it comes to reading the Bible. You will read terms like "sanctify", "reconciliation" or "redemption" and the first time you hear them you will say, "Wow, this is a confusing book. I don't understand!" or, "Boy, it is boring reading this Bible." But hang in there, the more you read the more it makes sense.

I can prove it right now; who do you root for, Michigan or Ohio State? Do you see how stirred up you get? The same will be true with His Word.

2. **Studying (Word, Topic, Book)**: Answering specifics

As you become familiar with the Bible, you will begin to start wanting to grow deeper in knowing it. God will put it on your heart to want to learn it because He wants you live off it. When I was growing up in my home my mom always made sure I had a nutritious meal and ate the right foods to have a balanced diet. Studying is the same thing. You must develop a way to learn God's full counsel. How does this relate to the following verse?

2 Timothy 2:15

And if you do, what is the result?

Psalm 19:7-11

So how do you study properly? There is no right or wrong way, but here is some help.

♦ A Word Study: This is studying a specific word that you have had some questions and confusion about.

◆ A Topical Study: This is studying a whole area that you are interested in--a person, place or concept.

◆ A Book Study: This is studying a whole book in the bible that you would like to know well.

If you need help in how to grow in depth in these areas ask the person you're studying the Bible with, which one has helped them. But remember, study the Bible in the way that is the most helpful for you to grow.

3. **Meditation**: Keeping a thought on your mind throughout the day

You may not know this, but a cow has three stomachs. You may be thinking, "So what?" Well, stay with me here. When a cow eats he starts chewing on the grass and then sends it to his first stomach to store it up. Then when he is hungry again he brings it up to his mouth again and chews. Then he sends it to stomach number two to store it. Once again he brings it up to chew, and then finally it goes to his third stomach to be sent on through digestion. This is what meditation is all about; you study the Bible, store it, bring the idea to mind again, then store it and bring to mind again. You do this until you really know a verse and it becomes a part of you. What do the following verses say. . .

Psalms 1:2

_____

_____

Psalm 119:15, 27, 48, 97, 148

_____

_____

_____

4. **Memorization**: To hide a specific verse, word for word, in your heart

This is a simple task that will allow you to have the Word of God everywhere you go without carrying a Bible. In fact, I have decided to memorize because I strongly believe that there could come a day when we will be put in jail for being a Christian, and even if I don't have a Bible in the jail cell, I will have it memorized in my mind. But that is the purpose, to have God's Word with you everywhere.

But what is the benefit to memorizing the Bible according to Psalm 119:11?

_____

_____

So, find a verse that you like and start memorizing it today-- and keep on doing it. You will be blessed by it!

▶ STEP THREE: Setting Up Your Own Biblical Diet

Before you go on, you must put down on paper (the next page) how you are going to set out to start studying the bible. Some of you may not have the slightest clue where to begin, so I will give you three tracks you can choose from. Remember, you don't have to pick any of these, but you need to start somewhere and this will help you get started.

1. TRACK ONE: Learning about Jesus

♦ Every day read three chapters without taking notes, you just want to read.

♦ Start with the book of Matthew, then Mark, then Luke and finish with John.

♦ Memorize one verse from each book you are reading per week

2. TRACK TWO: Learning about Christianity

♦ Every day study a paragraph and write down what you learn for the day.

♦ Some books to choose from are Romans (for heavy ideas), Philippians (for practical living) or James (for helpful advice).

♦ Memorize 2 verses a week from what you have studied.

3. TRACK THREE: Learning about salvation

◆ Find a book called a concordance and look up the words; Salvation, gospel, saved, redemption, reconciliation, born again.

◆ Write down every verse it lists on a piece of paper and study two verses a day by writing them down in your own words, and then writing what you think salvation means next to the verse.

◆ Memorize the verses you like the most and learn two a week.

♀ TAKE THE NEXT FIVE MINUTES TO DEVELOP YOUR OWN PLAN THAT YOU WILL START TOMORROW.

What type of study do you want to do?

What book of the Bible do you want to start in?

Are you going to memorize any verses during the week? Which ones and how many?

NOTES

Be a Berean!
Acts 17:11

WEEK THREE

Importance of Exercising

In last week's discussion, you were taught the importance of God's Word in the growth of your Christian walk and it is a great treasure. But a cancer has arisen in much of the Christian circles you will encounter. It is in the way they treat the Bible and I believe it is really distressing to God. There are many Christians that read and know God's Word, BUT THEY DON'T DO ANYTHING ABOUT IT! This is the essence of hypocrisy. If you hear the word hypocrite, how does it make you feel and why?

In fact, it is like eating a big turkey dinner at Thanksgiving; stuffing your belly with so much food that the only thing you are good for is sleeping on the couch or watching football. This is the way most Christians are in America; they are so stuffed with good Christian things that they just sit in the pews and go home. Lazy, fat and apathetic. As a new believer, you need to guard against this.

That is the purpose for this study: to help you understand fully. . .

▸ STEP ONE: The Danger of Getting Spiritually Fat

▸ STEP TWO: How to Spiritually Exercise

▸ STEP THREE: How to Incorporate the Bible into Your Life

▶ STEP ONE: The Danger of Getting Spiritually Fat

By the time you are done with week three, you will learn the proper perspective when it comes to living a life for Jesus. The sad part is, a majority of Christians have never learned these habits, but DON'T LET THAT HAPPEN TO YOU!

From the following verses, see if you can determine what you think God considers the necessary food you need to grow. . .

Matthew 4:4

1 Peter 2:2-3

1 Corinthians 3:1-2

Romans 10:17

♀ What is the food that God has provided for you?

In a show I used to watch, there was a robot that would always warn his family when there was danger approaching. He would say, "Warning, warning, warning! There is something that could destroy this family!" Well, in the same way, there is an attitude that could destroy your Christian walk, as it already has for so many Christians. I call it apathy. The following verses describe this condition. Put them into your own words. . .

James 1:22-25

Luke 4:46-49

Ezekiel 33:31-33

This section is intended to keep you aware of just how important God's Word is. If you don't treat it with respect, like a precious treasure, it will be taken away. Look at what Amos 8:11 says, and then put in your own words how you should treat God's Word?

▶ STEP TWO: How to Spiritually Exercise

Just as I am writing this paragraph I am looking at my large stomach. It is flabby, bulging out of my pants and causing me to be very down. All because I eat too much and don't exercise. If this continues much longer I will be no good to anyone but my fellow couch potatoes. This condition is not frowned upon too much in our culture anymore because most people are fat. But if we have this same attitude with our spiritual life, as we have just learned, God is not happy! We must exercise. . .

There are 3 main ways we spiritually exercise:

1. OBEY the Word

Read James 1:22 again and answer me this: "How do you not deceive yourself?"

What do you think it means, "to deceive yourself?"

According to John 14:23, how do we love God?

What do you think it means that God will come and make his home in us if we obey?

How do we become a friend of God according to John 15:14

In your own words, why is obedience so important?

Answer the following True or False:

♦ God wants us to obey because he delights in making life miserable for us. T F

♦ God wants us to obey because it is the only way we can earn his love. T F

♦ God wants us to obey because he loves us and he knows what really is best for us. T F

♦ God wants us to obey because he enjoys exerting power over weak humans. T F

♦ God wants us to obey because he wants us to stay stupid and ignorant; Spiritual brainwashing. T F

Hopefully, you said only answer 3 is true, but the sad thing is, most people deep down believe most of the lies. Do you know who is lying to us about not obeying God? What is the answer according to the following verses?

2 Corinthians 4:4

_____

_____

John 8:44

_____

_____

2 Thess. 2:9-12

_____

_____

Obedience does 4 things for you according to Proverbs 3:1-4. They are. . .

1. Prolonging your life

2. Bring you prosperity

3. Winning favor with God

4. Winning favor with man.

Do these four things sound like something you would like to have in your life?

2. SERVE others

Jesus gave us a great example of how to live, in fact, he showed us the Father perfectly, and if we follow his example we will do the will of God in our own life. One verse that I believe has enormous impact on a person's life is found in Matthew 20:28, what does it say?

Think about this verse, the King of the Universe didn't come for people to serve him hand and foot, but He served. Why would he do this?

Here are three reasons why we need to serve:

1. Philippians 2:1-4

(Hopefully, you said to bring unity in Christ)

2. 1 Corinthians 10:33

(Hopefully, you said to bring people to Christ)

3. 1 Peter 4:11:

_____

_____

(Hopefully, you said to bring praise for Christ)

Service is completely opposite of a world gone mad and when we serve, people will stand up and notice and we can then point them to Jesus! Take a look at 2 Timothy 3:1-5. . .

_____

_____

3. DECLARE the Gospel

When Jesus died, he immediately went up to heaven and left us down here on this earth. Why do you think he left the ones he loved back on this filthy planet?

Well, He tells us in the following verses:

John 17:13-18

_____

_____

_____

Acts 1:8

_____

_____

Acts 26:15-18

I grew up in a family of 8 and every Friday we would have pizza. When we were served the pizza all of us would have a slice, but can you imagine if my oldest brother were to hog all the pizza first and not let anyone else eat because he was strong? It would be terrible! Terrible because my parents gave us all pizza and for one person to hoard it would be complete selfishness. Well, the message of salvation was given to all people and when we don't share it, it is just like my brother not letting us have pizza.

In light of this last example, what does Paul mean by Romans 1:14-15?

What kind of a life did he live according to Acts 20:20-21?

What did he pray according to Ephesians 6:19?

PAUL REALLY KNEW HOW TO EXERCISE HIS FAITH!!!!!!

▶ STEP THREE: How to Incorporate the Bible into Your Life

This is where your faith really counts. If I believe a chair will hold me up the only way I prove it is if I sit down. If I believe that a certain woman is who I want to marry the only way to prove it is when I say, "I do". If I believe that Jesus is my God and I am a Christian the only way to prove it is if I live it. Read 1 John 3:18

SO LET'S PUT SHOE LEATHER TO OUR FAITH! In other words, here are 3 Practical Ways of how to daily live. . .

1. **Practical Ways to Obey the Word**

♦ JUST DO IT!

Read a verse and begin to live it. To take it a bit further, don't keep reading until the command becomes a habit.

♦ Observe God's Ordinances (specific commands from Jesus)

Are you baptized? God commands it. If not, talk to a Pastor immediately. Are you participating in communion? If not, join a church immediately.

♦ Listen very intently to Sunday preaching.

This will be a way that God confronts you directly with what you are doing right or wrong. Buy a journal to write down what you learn at church.

2. Practical Ways to Serve Others

♦ Get involved in a church body.

You should contact a local pastor and ask them how you can start being used at a good church.

♦ Learn about spiritual gifts according to. . .

    Ephesians 4:11-12

    Romans 12:3-8

    1 Corinthians 12:12-26

You have been given a gift from God to use in a local church body. To help the name of Christ to be glorified, your gift needs to be used. To find it out, learn of these gifts and then find a church to see how they are carried out in your life.

♦ Ask God to give you a heart for people's needs around you.

Read Isaiah 50:4 and answer this; why does God give the writer an instructed tongue?

_____

_____

_____

(Hopefully, you said to know the Word that sustains the weary)

Who is weary around you? As you look for them God will prepare you to serve them.

3. Practical Ways to Declare the Gospel

♦ Pray for 5 people daily you know who don't know Jesus. Who are they?

1. _____
2. _____
3. _____
4. _____
5. _____

As you pray for those people, look for opportunities to present the gospel to them. To help you with this, memorize Colossians 4:2-6 to help guide your steps.

♦ Learn the Roman Road

To share the gospel with people at any time, anywhere, and any situation, cut out the square in the back of the book to bring with you.

♀ The Roman Road is one way to easily share the gospel. But as you learn more scripture the easier to share the truth of Christ will be.

If you practically apply what you have learned this week, you will start to please God like few Christians do these days! One last question to think about for the week:

IF YOU WERE REALLY SAVED FROM HELL, ETERNAL TORMENT, BY THE DEATH OF JESUS, THEN SHOULD IT BE TOO MUCH TO ASK US TO "DENY OURSELVES, PICK UP OUR CROSS AND FOLLOW HIM"?

If the answer is "no" then we have no other choice but to EXERCISE OUR FAITH!

WEEK FOUR

Importance of Spiritual Rest

Do you hear him? "Ha, ha, ha! You have become a Christian, huh? Well, it won't last long. Sure, you got all excited by some fancy speaker, or maybe you had one bad turn in the road and you needed help, but don't worry, this feeling will pass. You will get tired of living for this so-called Jesus and you will go back to your old way of living again!"

Have these thoughts crept up into your head since you have made the choice to follow Jesus? Look at 2 Timothy 3:12, what does it say? So, in other words, don't be surprised if the devil is going to try to discourage you, ridicule you, and try to stop you from following fully after Jesus. Has he started to pull at you yet? If so, how does it feel?

There are three steps in order to stay strong for Christ…

▸ STEP ONE: We Need Our Rest

▸ STEP TWO: How to Pray

▸ STEP THREE: Final Commitment

▶ STEP ONE: We Need Our Rest

By the time you are done with this week four, you should be able to live for Jesus guilt-free. The goal of Christianity is to "Be With God", not "Be Religious." That is the goal.

This will not be a long study this week, in fact, we are just going to learn 2 things.

1. What it means to spiritually rest
2. How we rest

You need a rest from work, from people and from sports, but rest in the physical sense is the absence of an activity. However, Biblical rest is not getting rid of something, it really is adding something and it can be found in this one simple but profound verse. . .

Matthew 11:28-30

1. Who do we go to to get rest?

2. What does Jesus ask us to do to get rest?

3. What in the world do you think that means?

Jesus is using the illustration of a yoke as an example to say, "When you come to me, you will be yoked up with me. I will do the pulling and you follow." How strong is Jesus?

How does this story relate to this verse: 2 Corinthians 12:9-10?

So when living for Christ starts to get hard, painful and even to the point of suffering, how are we supposed to live?

Do you think that is easy to do? Why or why not?

How to practically do this? How do we rest? One word. . .

PRAY

▶ STEP TWO: How to Pray

Prayer is how we rest. Look what I mean. . .

1. When Satan attacks (1 Peter 5:8) and I am getting worn out, how do I get relief and rest from him?

James 4:7

Ephesians 6:18

2. When the situation I am in seems so confusing and I don't know what to do, how do I rest?

Philippians 4:6

Romans 8:26

Hebrews 4:14-16

3. When I have so many troubles surrounding me and I don't know which way to turn, how do I rest?

James 1:2-6

James 4:1-3

4. What do I do when I need something and I am so worried that I won't get it, how do I rest?

Matthew 7:7-12

SO HOW DO I PRAY?

It seems so hard, how do I really talk to the Creator of the universe?

I LIKE TO MAKE THINGS SIMPLE, AND USABLE.

1. Set aside a time, a daily time to meet with God.
    ♦ Earlier the better
    ♦ Set at least 10 minutes to pray
    ♦ Be consistent, DON'T GIVE UP!

2. Just plain talk to God, be real and be yourself.

3. Use the bible to help you pray.
    ♦ Pray through the Psalms
    ♦ Have your bible leader share his prayer life.

Really, I have no more to say about prayer because prayer is just a relationship between you and God. After you start growing in Christ you can learn more about prayer, but the key is just to start praying. Talk to Him, and learn to fall in love with Him.

Dear Lord Jesus Christ,

I commit to start praying daily, help me Holy Spirit

Signed: _____

❖ If you need additional help understanding the Bible, we recommend the next booklet in the New Believer's Series, Bible Toolkit, which can also be purchased at:

www.christopherjweeks.com

THE ROMAN ROAD

1. Romans 3:23 – All men sin

2. Romans 6:23 – Sin leads to death (hell too!)

3. Romans 5:8 – Jesus paid for our sin

4. Romans 10:9-10 – Believe and confess for true salvation

5. John 5:24 – If you believe it you are in heaven

ALSO AVAILABLE

BIBLE
TOOLKIT
A NEW BELIEVERS GUIDE TO THE BIBLE

christopher j weeks

Made in the USA
Coppell, TX
21 May 2021